second edition

emotionally intelligent leadership

for Students

Inventory

**Marcy Levy Shankman,
Scott J. Allen, and
Rosanna Miguel**

JOSSEY-BASS™
A Wiley Brand

Published by Jossey-Bass
A Wiley Brand
One Montgomery Street, Suite 1000, San Francisco, CA 94104-4594
www.josseybass.com/highereducation

Jossey-Bass books and products are available through most bookstores. To contact Jossey-Bass directly call our Customer Care Department within the U.S. at 800-956-7739, outside the U.S. at 317-572-3986, or fax 317-572-4002.

Wiley publishes in a variety of print and electronic formats and by print-on-demand. Some material included with standard print versions of this book may not be included in e-books or in print-on-demand. If this book refers to media such as a CD or DVD that is not included in the version you purchased, you may download this material at http://booksupport.wiley.com. For more information about Wiley products, visit www.wiley.com.

ISBN: 978-1-118-82166-4 (paper), 978-1-118-97379-0 (ebk.), 978-1-118-97378-3 (ebk.)

Printed in the United States of America
SECOND EDITION

PB Printing 10 9 8 7 6 5 4

Introduction

Emotionally intelligent leadership (EIL) promotes an intentional focus on three facets: consciousness of self, consciousness of others, and consciousness of context. Across the three EIL facets are nineteen capacities that equip individuals with the knowledge, skills, perspectives, and attitudes to achieve desired leadership outcomes.

Before you begin, consider a few of our basic assumptions about leadership:

- Leadership is available to all of us.
- Leadership can be learned.
- Leadership is art and science.
- Leadership requires inner work.

Each one of these assumptions provides a core part of the foundation for EIL. You'll notice we didn't say you had to have a formal title or position to lead others. Sometimes you make a conscious decision to pursue a leadership role; other times the opportunity simply presents itself and you step up. Either way, we agree with Joseph Rost (1993), who suggests that leadership is "an influence relationship among leaders and followers who intend real changes that reflect their mutual purposes" (p. 102). In other words, leaders and followers often collaborate toward a common end point.

Each of us, often on a moment's notice, move from leader to follower (and vice versa) depending on the context. So we suggest that leaders *and* followers can behave in an emotionally intelligent manner. Thus, it's not just about emotionally intelligent leadership; it's also about emotionally intelligent followership.

Instructions: This self-assessment gives you an opportunity to learn more about yourself and better understand how you lead others. The best insight will come when

- you are honest with yourself;
- you respond to the questions based on who you are today, not on who you hope to become; and
- you respond to the statements quickly—try not to analyze them.

Use the rating numbers shown. Indicate the extent to which you *intentionally* do the following:

Never	Almost Never	Rarely	Sometimes	Usually	Almost Always	Always
1	2	3	4	5	6	7

When serving in a formal or informal leadership role, I ...

1.	Recognize how situations influence my emotions	1	2	3	4	5	**6**	7
2.	Stay calm in challenging situations	1	2	3	4	5	**6**	7
3.	Am honest about my intentions	1	2	3	4	5	6	**7**
4.	Believe in my skills	1	2	3	4	5	**6**	7
5.	Am open to change	1	2	3	4	5	**6**	7
6.	Present a positive outlook	1	2	3	4	5	**6**	7
7.	Act before someone tells me to	1	2	3	4	5	6	**7**
8.	Establish personal standards for myself	1	2	3	4	5	6	**7**
9.	Place a high value on the feelings of others	1	2	3	4	5	**6**	7
10.	Communicate an exciting vision	1	2	3	4	**5**	6	7
11.	Help others realize their potential	1	2	3	4	5	**6**	7
12.	Demonstrate an appreciation for cultural diversity	1	2	3	4	5	**6**	7
13.	Build relationships with ease	1	2	3	4	5	**6**	7
14.	Emphasize team goals	1	2	3	4	5	**6**	7
15.	Fulfill my responsibilities to others	1	2	3	4	5	6	**7**
16.	Address difficult situations effectively	1	2	3	4	**5**	6	7
17.	Promote innovative thinking	1	2	3	4	5	**6**	7
18.	Respond effectively to the group	1	2	3	4	5	**6**	7
19.	Intentionally alter my approach to leadership to meet the needs of the situation	1	2	3	4	5	6	**7**
20.	Recognize how my emotions influence my actions	1	2	3	4	5	6	**7**
21.	Remain calm in stressful situations	1	2	3	4	5	**6**	7
22.	Present my motives in an honest manner	1	2	3	4	5	6	**7**
23.	Demonstrate confidence	1	2	3	4	5	**6**	7
24.	Adapt my behavior to changing situations	1	2	3	4	5	**6**	7

Never	Almost Never	Rarely	Sometimes	Usually	Almost Always	Always
1	2	3	4	5	6	7

When serving in a formal or informal leadership role, I ...

25.	Foster a sense of hope	1	2	3	4	5	(6)	7
26.	Take advantage of opportunities that come my way	1	2	3	4	5	(6)	7
27.	Strive to improve based on my personal standards	1	2	3	4	5	6	(7)
28.	Show concerns for the feelings of others	1	2	3	4	5	6	(7)
29.	Inspire commitment to the group's vision	1	2	3	4	5	6	(7)
30.	Help others enhance their abilities	1	2	3	4	5	(6)	7
31.	Find common ground among different points of view	1	2	3	4	5	(6)	7
32.	Create connections with others easily	1	2	3	4	5	(6)	7
33.	Build strong teams	1	2	3	4	5	(6)	7
34.	Follow through on my commitments to the group	1	2	3	4	5	6	(7)
35.	Address conflict with individuals effectively	1	2	3	4	5	(6)	7
36.	Seek to improve upon the status quo when future gains can be made	1	2	3	4	5	6	(7)
37.	Follow the established rules of the group	1	2	3	4	5	(6)	7
38.	Adapt my approach to leadership based on the situation	1	2	3	4	5	(6)	7
39.	Recognize how my emotions affect me	1	2	3	4	5	(6)	7
40.	Maintain composure	1	2	3	4	5	(6)	7
41.	Act genuinely	1	2	3	4	5	6	(7)
42.	Remain confident when facing challenges	1	2	3	4	5	(6)	7
43.	Am open to changing my opinion	1	2	3	4	5	(6)	7
44.	Communicate a positive outlook	1	2	3	4	5	6	(7)
45.	Take advantage of new opportunities	1	2	3	4	5	6	(7)
46.	Establish high personal standards for myself	1	2	3	4	5	6	(7)
47.	Respond to the emotional needs of others	1	2	3	4	5	(6)	7
48.	Inspire commitment to the group's mission	1	2	3	4	5	(6)	7
49.	Create opportunities for others to learn	1	2	3	4	5	(6)	7
50.	Appreciate individual differences	1	2	3	4	5	(6)	7
51.	Build a strong network of relationships	1	2	3	4	5	(6)	7
52.	Work well with others toward a shared goal	1	2	3	4	5	(6)	7
53.	Recognize a need to give to the group	1	2	3	4	5	(6)	7
54.	Manage conflict effectively	1	2	3	4	(5)	6	7
55.	Consider ways to improve the group's performance through innovation	1	2	3	4	5	6	(7)
56.	Align my actions with the values of the group	1	2	3	4	5	(6)	7
57.	Learn about what it takes to succeed in different settings	1	2	3	4	5	(6)	7

Results

Step 1: Scoring

Transfer your ratings to the corresponding statement numbers here. Add the numbers across each row to determine your total for each capacity.

	Statement Numbers			Total	
Emotional Self-Perception	1. 6	20. 7	39. 6	19	= ESP
Emotional Self-Control	2. 6	21. 6	40. 6	18	= ESC
Authenticity ✳	3. 7	22. 7	41. 7	21	= AU
Healthy Self-Esteem	4. 4	23. 6	42. 6	18	= HSE
Flexibility ✳	5. 6	24. 6	43. 6	18	= FL
Optimism	6. 6	25. 6	44. 4	18	= OP
Initiative ✳	7. 7	26. 6	45. 7	20	= IN
Achievement ✳	8. 7	27. 7	46. 7	21	= AC
Displaying Empathy	9. 6	28. 7	47. 6	19	= DE
Inspiring Others	10. 5	29. 7	48. 6	18	= IO

	Statement Numbers			Total	
Coaching Others	11. 6	30. 6	49. 6	18	= CO
Capitalizing on Difference	12. 6	31. 6	50. 6	18	= CD
Developing Relationships	13. 6	32. 6	51. 6	18	= DR
Building Teams	14. 6	33. 6	52. 6	18	= BT
Demonstrating Citizenship	15. 7	34. 7	53. 6	20	= DC
Managing Conflict ✓	16. 5	35. 6	54. 5	16	= MC
Facilitating Change	17. 6	36. 7	55. 7	20	= FC
Analyzing the Group	18. 6	37. 6	56. 6	18	= AG
Assessing the Environment	19. 7	38. 6	57. 6	19	= AE

Step 2: EIL Line Chart

Plot your total scores on the chart following, indicating with a dot on the corresponding line your total score for each capacity. Once all the scores have been plotted, connect each dot to make a line chart.

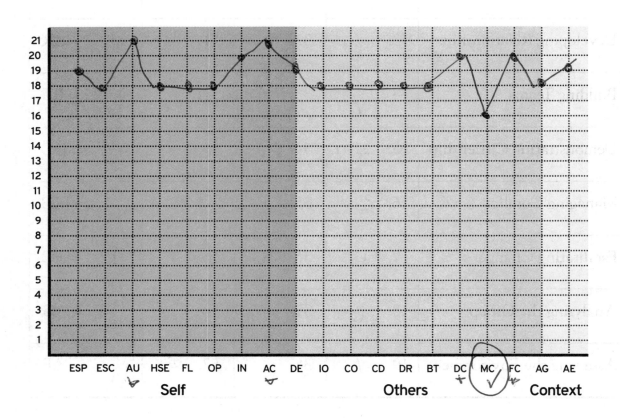

Step 3: Interpretation

As described in the introduction, we identify three facets of EIL: consciousness of self, consciousness of others, and consciousness of context.

1. *Consciousness of self:* Demonstrating emotionally intelligent leadership involves awareness of your abilities, emotions, and perceptions. Consciousness of self is about prioritizing

the inner work of reflection and introspection and appreciating that self-awareness is a continual and ongoing process. *Emotionally intelligent leaders are self-aware.*

2. *Consciousness of others:* Demonstrating emotionally intelligent leadership involves awareness of the abilities, emotions, and perceptions of others. Consciousness of others is about intentionally working with and influencing individuals and groups to bring about positive change. *Emotionally intelligent leaders energize, influence, and engage others.*

3. *Consciousness of context:* Demonstrating emotionally intelligent leadership involves awareness of the setting and situation. Consciousness of context is about paying attention to how environmental factors and internal group dynamics affect the process of leadership. *Emotionally intelligent leaders understand that what works in one instance will not necessarily be effective in another.*

Housed under these three facets are nineteen capacities. We define *capacity* as the ability to execute or perform. A strong command of the nineteen capacities can assist you in achieving desired results in a leadership context.

1. The nineteen capacities are defined in the appendix. Please read these and **star** (★) those that you think, **in a general sense**, are strengths and place a **checkmark** (✓) next to those that you think are areas for development.

2. On your EIL Line Chart, **star** (★) your three highest capacity scores and re-read the capacity definitions in the appendix. These represent the capacities in which you perceive yourself to have the greatest strengths.

3. Likewise, place a **checkmark** (✓) next to your three lowest capacity scores and re-read the capacity definitions in the appendix. These represent the capacities in which you perceive yourself to have the greatest room for growth.

Next Steps

Recognize that the nineteen capacities are tools for you to use. Each one of us has different levels of awareness, comfort, and proficiency with each of the capacities. It's likely that you rely on certain capacities more than others because they come naturally to you. Many capacities we learn and develop over time. Through reflection and feedback, you can deepen your understanding of your strengths and areas for growth. But how do you develop your capacities?

For starters, write your full signature in cursive with your *nondominant* hand in the space provided.

For most of us, the signature will look like that of a young child. However, you can learn to write with your nondominant hand with intentional practice. Most likely, using your nondominant hand did not feel comfortable, but over time, and with additional practice, you could improve your signature.

The same is true of developing your EIL capacities. Taking a strength and making it even better, or improving on an area of growth, takes time, practice, and dedication. At first, using some capacities may be uncomfortable or difficult (e.g., you may not see yourself as inspiring to others). As you continue to practice, receive feedback, and reflect, those capacities will feel more natural. As we know, development requires experience, focus, and an intentional commitment to improvement.

Synthesis

Based on your results in the previous section, identify one area of strength (a capacity that you think you are best at demonstrating consistently) and one area for development (a capacity that you think you could improve) for each of the three EIL facets (self, others, context). *These choices may correspond to the capacities you identified as strengths and areas for development, but they do not have to. The choice is yours—what you select should feel powerful and important to you.*

Consciousness of Self
1. Area of strength: Capacity of *Achievement*
2. Area of development: Capacity of *Optimism*

Consciousness of Others
1. Area of strength: Capacity of *Facilitating Change*
2. Area of development: Capacity of *Managing Conflict*

Consciousness of Context
1. Area of strength: Capacity of *Assessing Environment*
2. Area of development: Capacity of *Analyzing the Group*

Finally, of the capacities identified, circle *one* that you believe, if mastered, will have the greatest impact on your development. Keep this capacity in mind as you complete the next section.

Suggestions for Development

Regardless of which capacity you selected, consider the following general suggestions.

First, let a mentor or friend know that you want to improve. By doing so, you invite this person to help, and hold you accountable. Sharing with others that you want to improve can be challenging because it places you in a vulnerable position. However, when others know you're trying to develop a skill, they tend to be more understanding of mistakes. They may also be more interested in helping you learn. Think about how athletes or musicians place themselves in the same position. To excel and develop their skills, they must practice and be open to feedback from their coach. Many would agree that professional tennis player Serena Williams has incredible natural ability, but she needed people like her father, her sister, and others (teachers, coaches, mentors) along the way to guide her to the next level. Who is guiding you?

Second, we suggest placing yourself in environments in which you can practice the capacity you hope to develop. We call these *edge* experiences. You know you are at your *edge* when you have a nervous feeling in your stomach—a feeling of uncertainty as to how things will turn out. For some, this may be managing conflict; for others, it may be building a team. Being at the edge requires some risk taking. What is your edge? What experience(s) will help take your abilities to a new level? Who can help you along the way? Clarity around these questions is paramount as you strive to develop.

The key is *intentionality*. In other words, just as with any other skill, you have to *want* to develop it. Effective leadership takes commitment and awareness. Leadership development requires changes in behavior. You must expect to practice and take some risks if you want to improve your knowledge, skills, and abilities.

The following list offers *potential* ways to develop the capacity you identified. We all learn and develop in different ways. Read each suggestion and place a star next to the two or three ideas that best fit your learning style. If you have additional ideas, there is room at the end to insert them.

Development Ideas

1. Locate and meet with a mentor who has mastered the capacity.

2. Read an article or book on the capacity you hope to develop.

3. Join an organization (e.g., campus, community, professional association) or place yourself in situations that require you to practice the capacity.

4. Take part in formal learning opportunities, retreats, or courses that feature the capacity.

5. Blog or journal about the process of developing the capacity. Comment on where you see it, who does it well, who struggles with it, and so on.

6. Have coffee or otherwise connect with people working on the same capacity and talk about your experience(s).

7. Write a vision statement or story about a future positive state as it relates to the capacity. What will it look like when you have mastered this capacity? Who will you become? What will it allow you to accomplish?

8. Participate in opportunities that allow you to teach others about the capacity you wish to develop.

9. Complete an assessment or instrument that can help you learn more about your strengths and areas for growth.

10. Search the Web for resources and tools that may help you develop the capacity.

11. Talk with friends who know you well and ask them to suggest, based on their knowledge of you, how you can best develop the capacity.

12. Seek out work opportunities that will require you to use and practice the capacity you wish to develop.

Development Ideas (*continued*)

13. Sign up for an online course (through your institution or the many free courses available on the Web).

14. Do activities in the *EILS: Student Workbook, Second Edition*, that are focused on the capacity you wish to develop.

15. Create an online community or learning space on the capacity of interest.

16. Other:

17. Other:

18. Other:

Conclusion

Leadership is complex. Remember that developing EIL will keep you in a continual state of investigation. The relationships among consciousness of self, consciousness of others, and consciousness of context are ever-changing. What works in one situation may not work in another. What was successful last week may not be successful next week. Likewise, in some situations you may need to demonstrate one combination of capacities, whereas another situation may call for a completely different combination to yield success. To better understand EIL, we suggest reading *Emotionally Intelligent Leadership: A Guide for Students, Second Edition* and completing the activities in the *Student Workbook, Second Edition*.

Finally, leadership development is an intentional process. By choosing one capacity to focus on, you have begun a process that can be replicated as you continue to facilitate your growth and development. Leadership development is an ongoing and iterative process. When you are ready, revisit this resource and choose another capacity to develop. To close, keep in mind the words of legendary UCLA basketball coach John Wooden:

> Success is peace of mind which is a direct result of self-satisfaction in knowing you did your best to become the best you are capable of becoming.

Reference

Rost, J. (1993). *Leadership for the twenty-first century.* Westport, CT: Praeger.

Appendix A EIL Overview

Emotionally intelligent leadership (EIL) promotes an intentional focus on three facets: consciousness of self, consciousness of others, and consciousness of context. Across the three EIL facets are nineteen capacities that equip individuals with the knowledge, skills, perspectives, and attitudes to achieve desired leadership outcomes.

🛜 Consciousness of Self

Demonstrating emotionally intelligent leadership involves awareness of your abilities, emotions, and perceptions. Consciousness of self is about prioritizing the inner work of reflection and introspection, and appreciating that self-awareness is a continual and ongoing process.

- *Emotional Self-Perception:* <u>Identifying emotions and their impact on behavior.</u> Emotional self-perception is about describing, naming, and understanding your emotions. Emotionally intelligent leaders are aware of how situations influence emotions and how emotions affect interactions with others.
- *Emotional Self-Control:* <u>Consciously moderating emotions.</u> Emotional self-control means intentionally managing your emotions and understanding how and when to demonstrate them appropriately. Emotionally intelligent leaders take responsibility for regulating their emotions and are not victims of them.
- *Authenticity:* <u>Being transparent and trustworthy.</u> Authenticity is about developing credibility, being transparent, and aligning words with actions. Emotionally intelligent leaders live their values and present themselves and their motives in an open and honest manner.
- *Healthy Self-Esteem:* <u>Having a balanced sense of self.</u> Healthy self-esteem is about balancing confidence in your abilities

with humility. Emotionally intelligent leaders are resilient and remain confident when faced with setbacks and challenges.

- *Flexibility*: <u>Being open and adaptive to change.</u> Flexibility is about adapting your approach and style based on changing circumstances. Emotionally intelligent leaders seek input and feedback from others and adjust accordingly.
- *Optimism*: <u>Having a positive outlook.</u> Optimism is about setting a positive tone for the future. Emotionally intelligent leaders use optimism to foster hope and generate energy.
- *Initiative*: <u>Taking action.</u> Initiative means being a self-starter and being motivated to take the first step. Emotionally intelligent leaders are ready to take action, demonstrate interest, and capitalize on opportunities.
- *Achievement*: <u>Striving for excellence.</u> Achievement is about setting high personal standards and getting results. Emotionally intelligent leaders strive to improve and are motivated by an internal drive to succeed.

🛜 Consciousness of Others

Demonstrating emotionally intelligent leadership involves awareness of the abilities, emotions, and perceptions of others. Consciousness of others is about intentionally working with and influencing individuals and groups to bring about positive change.

- *Displaying Empathy*: <u>Being emotionally in tune with others.</u> Empathy is about perceiving and addressing the emotions of others. Emotionally intelligent leaders place a high value on the feelings of others and respond to their emotional cues.
- *Inspiring Others*: <u>Energizing individuals and groups.</u> Inspiration occurs when people are excited about a better future. Emotionally intelligent leaders foster feelings of enthusiasm and commitment to organizational mission, vision, and goals.

- *Coaching   Others:* <u>Enhancing the skills and abilities of others.</u> Coaching is about helping *others* enhance their skills, talents, and abilities. Emotionally intelligent leaders know they cannot do everything themselves and create opportunities for others to develop.

- *Capitalizing on Difference:* <u>Benefiting from multiple perspectives.</u> Capitalizing on difference means recognizing our unique identities, perspectives, and experiences are assets, not barriers. Emotionally intelligent leaders appreciate and use difference as an opportunity to create a broader perspective.

- *Developing Relationships:* <u>Building a network of trusting relationships.</u> Developing relationships means creating meaningful connections. Emotionally intelligent leaders encourage opportunities for relationships to grow and develop.

- *Building Teams:* <u>Working with others to accomplish a shared purpose.</u> Building teams is about effectively communicating, creating a shared purpose, and clarifying roles to get results. Emotionally intelligent leaders foster group cohesion and develop a sense of "we."

- *Demonstrating Citizenship:* <u>Fulfilling responsibilities to the group.</u> Citizenship is about being actively engaged and following through on your commitments. Emotionally intelligent leaders meet their ethical and moral obligations for the benefit of others and the larger purpose.

- *Managing Conflict:* <u>Identifying and resolving conflict.</u> Managing conflict is about working through differences to facilitate the group process. Emotionally intelligent leaders skillfully and confidently address conflicts to find the best solution.

- *Facilitating Change:* <u>Working toward new directions.</u> Facilitating change is about advancing ideas and initiatives through innovation and creativity. Emotionally intelligent leaders seek to improve on the status quo and mobilize others toward a better future.

🛜 Consciousness of Context

Demonstrating emotionally intelligent leadership involves awareness of the setting and situation. Consciousness of context is about paying attention to how environmental factors and internal group dynamics affect the process of leadership.

- *Analyzing the Group:* Interpreting group dynamics. Analyzing the group is about recognizing that values, rules, rituals, and internal politics play a role in every group. Emotionally intelligent leaders know how to diagnose, interpret, and address these dynamics.
- *Assessing the Environment:* Interpreting external forces and trends. Assessing the environment is about recognizing the social, cultural, economic, and political forces that influence leadership. Emotionally intelligent leaders use their awareness of the external environment to lead effectively.

If you enjoyed this book, you may also like these:

**Emotionally Intelligent
Leadership for Students:
Student Workbook,
2nd Edition
by Marcy Levy Shankman,
Scott J. Allen, Paige Haber-Curran**
ISBN: 9781118821824

**Emotionally Intelligent
Leadership for Students:
Facilitation and Activity Guide,
2nd Edition
by Marcy Levy Shankman,
Scott J. Allen, Paige Haber-Curran**
ISBN: 9781118821770

**Emotionally Intelligent
Leadership: A Guide for
Students, 2nd Edition
by Marcy Levy Shankman,
Scott J. Allen,
Paige Haber-Curran**
ISBN: 9781118821787

WILEY

Want to connect?

Like us on Facebook
https://www.facebook.com/JBHigherEd

Follow us on Twitter
https://twitter.com/JBHigherEd

WILEY

TOP NOTCH 1

TEACHER TIPS

ALL ACROSS THE CURRICULUM

**EDITED BY
ROSEMARY ALEXANDER**

SCHOLASTIC
PROFESSIONAL BOOKS

New York • Toronto • London • Auckland • Sydney

Designed by Intergraphics
Cover design by Vincent Ceci
Illustrations by Terri Chicko, Joe Chicko, Michelle Fridkin

ISBN 0-590-49098-2